TINY BUGS
UP CLOSE

Gareth Stevens
Publishing

BY JANEY LEVY

Please visit our website, www.garethstevens.com. For a free color catalog of all our high-quality books, call toll free 1-800-542-2595 or fax 1-877-542-2596.

Library of Congress Cataloging-in-Publication Data

Levy, Janey.
 Tiny bugs up close / Janey Levy.
     p. cm. — (Under the microscope)
 Includes index.
 ISBN 978-1-4339-8351-1 (pbk.)
 ISBN 978-1-4339-8352-8 (6-pack)
 ISBN 978-1-4339-8350-4 (library binding)
 1. Insects—Juvenile literature. 2. Microscopy—Juvenile literature. 3. Microbiology—
Juvenile literature. I. Title. II. Series: Under the microscope.
 QL467.2.L48 2014
 595.02—dc23

                                        2012047156

First Edition

Published in 2014 by
Gareth Stevens Publishing
111 East 14th Street, Suite 349
New York, NY 10003

Copyright © 2014 Gareth Stevens Publishing

Designer: Katelyn E. Reynolds
Editor: Therese Shea

Photo credits: Cover, p. 1 Derek Berwin/The Image Bank/Getty Images; cover, pp. 1, 3–31 (logo and bug image icon) iStockphoto/Thinkstock.com; cover, pp. 1–31 (bug image icons) Jubal Harshaw/Shutterstock.com; cover, pp. 1–31 (bug image icon) Sebastian Kaulitzki/Shutterstock.com; cover, pp. 1–31 (bug image icon) Juan Gaertner/ Shutterstock.com; cover, pp. 1–32 (background texture) Hemera/Thinkstock.com; p. 5 Doug Martin/Photo Researcher/Getty Images; p. 6 S. E. Thorpe/Wikipedia.com; pp. 7, 10, 12, 15 iStockphoto/Thinkstock.com; p. 9 Mariana Ruiz Villarreal LadyofHats/ Wikipedia.com; p. 11 Dorling Kindersley/the Agency Collection/Getty Images; p. 13 Visuals Unlimited, Inc./Robert Pickett/Getty Images; pp. 14, 23 (main) Steve Gschmeissner/Science Photo Library/Getty Images; p. 17 RMF/Visuals Unlimited/ Getty Images; p. 19 Luc Viatour/www.lucnix.be/Wikipedia.com; p. 21 Tim Flach/ Stone/Getty Images; p. 23 (inset) CDC/Janice Haney Carr; p. 25 Nature's Images/ Photo Researchers/Getty Images; p. 27 Brian0918/Wikipedia.com; p. 29 Justin Black/ Shutterstock.com.

Printed in the United States of America

CPSIA compliance information: Batch #CS13GS: For further information contact Gareth Stevens, New York, New York at 1-800-542-2595.

CONTENTS

The World of Bugs 4

Menacing Mosquitoes 8

Feasting Fleas 12

Nibbling No-See-Ums 16

Mite-y Chiggers 18

Lousy Lice 20

Skin Eaters 22

Pantry Pests 24

Earth Alert! 26

Beneficial Bugs 28

Glossary 30

For More Information 31

Index 32

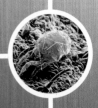

Words in the glossary appear in **bold** type
the first time they are used in the text.

THE WORLD OF BUGS

DID YOU KNOW?

It would take more than 6,000 pages in a book to list the scientific names of all the known insect species.

We like to think of humans as the most successful animal on Earth. There are more than 7 billion people on Earth. They live in all sorts of **environments** all over the planet. But did you know the same number of insects occupies each square mile (2.6 sq km) of land? That equals almost 400 **quadrillion** insects on Earth—about 57 million times the number of people!

Scientists have identified more than 1.5 million species, or kinds, of animals. About 1 million of these are insects, and scientists discover thousands more species every year. Some believe there could be more than 10 million insect species. And, like people, insects live almost everywhere on Earth. Only the oceans have small numbers of insects.

ADAPTED TO
SUCCEED

Insects have adapted to live in any environment where they can find food. They live in tropical rainforests and dry deserts. They live in polar regions, on glaciers, and in caves deep in the earth. You can find them in cold mountain streams and in hot springs. Some even live in pools of raw petroleum, or oil, where they eat other insects that fall in.

Some people collect insects. Since there are about a million insect species that we know of, collections can be quite large!

THE TEENY, TINY
FAIRY FLY

Fairy flies are among the smallest insects in the world. They're only about 0.01 inch (0.25 mm) long. That means they're small enough to go through the eye of a needle! There are more than 1,400 species of these tiny insects, and, in spite of their name, they aren't really flies. They're **parasitic** wasps that lay their eggs inside other insects' eggs. When the wasp larvae hatch, they eat the host insect still growing in its egg!

Many kinds of fairy flies have wings like the one pictured here.

People also apply the term "bugs" to creatures such as spiders, ticks, and mites. These animals are arachnids, not insects. Insects have an **exoskeleton**, three main body parts, six legs, and antennae, or feelers. Most have wings, too. Arachnids also have an exoskeleton, but they have two main body parts, eight legs, and no antennae or wings. About 90,000 arachnid species exist worldwide.

When people think of bugs, they often picture creatures such as bumblebees, grasshoppers, butterflies, and large spiders such as tarantulas. But most insects are less than 0.25 inch (6.4 mm) long. And arachnids can be as small as 0.003 inch (0.08 mm) long! The smallest bugs are difficult to see without a microscope. But they can have a big effect on our lives.

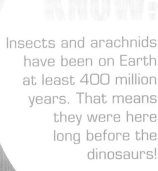

DID YOU KNOW?

Insects and arachnids have been on Earth at least 400 million years. That means they were here long before the dinosaurs!

wood tick

MENACING MOSQUITOES

DID YOU KNOW?

Mosquitoes belong to the large group of insects called flies. In fact, *mosquito* is Spanish for "little fly."

No matter where you live, you've probably had experiences with mosquitoes—and their bites. Worldwide, over 3,000 mosquito species exist. Most are only about 0.25 inch (6.4 mm) long. But in spite of their tiny size, some can be deadly. Their bite can transmit diseases such as malaria, yellow fever, and West Nile virus.

You might be surprised to learn that only female mosquitoes bite. And the blood they drink from their victims isn't food for them. They need it to help the eggs inside their body develop. Food for adult mosquitoes comes from plant juices.

Most of us quickly brush a mosquito away when we hear the hum of its beating wings or feel it bite. But a close look reveals a rather amazing creature.

A MOSQUITO'S BODY

Most mosquitoes are black, brown, gray, or tan, although a few are bright blue or green. Thin scales and fine, threadlike structures cover the mosquito's body and wings. Veins carry blood to the thin wings and stiffen and support them. Holes called spiracles run along the sides of the body and allow the mosquito to breathe. A pair of claws on each leg lets the mosquito cling to flat surfaces.

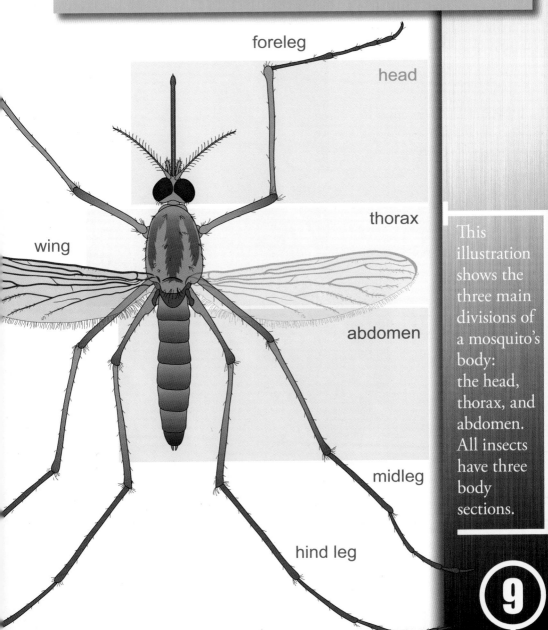

foreleg

head

wing

thorax

abdomen

midleg

hind leg

This illustration shows the three main divisions of a mosquito's body: the head, thorax, and abdomen. All insects have three body sections.

GOTCHA!

Different mosquito species prefer the blood of different animals. How do they find their victims? Mosquitoes have many ways. Their antennae can detect the **carbon dioxide** animals breathe out from 164 feet (50 m) away. They can also detect **lactic acid** in sweat. Mosquitoes' vision isn't very good, but they can easily see movement. In addition, they can detect heat. With all these abilities, it's no wonder they're so good at finding victims!

This amazing close-up clearly shows the mosquito's compound eyes and the proboscis piercing the skin. OUCH!

A mosquito's head—the body section that delivers the annoying bite—is fascinating up close. Two huge compound eyes, each made of thousands of lenses, cover most of the head. Between the eyes are two antennae, which the insect uses to hear and smell.

A mosquito's mouth is funnel shaped and lacks jaws. That means a female mosquito can't really bite her victims. Instead, she pierces the skin using a tubelike part called the proboscis that extends down from the mouth. Inside the proboscis are six needlelike parts called stylets. The female mosquito stabs her victim's skin with these. Mosquito saliva, or spit, flows into the wound to keep the blood from clotting. Then, the insect uses her proboscis like a straw to suck up blood!

FEASTING FLEAS

DID YOU KNOW?

More than 94 percent of flea species feed on mammals. The remainder feed on birds.

If you have a cat or dog—or even a pet rat—you're probably familiar with fleas. You may even have shared the misery of fleabites with your pet. These bloodsucking parasites are quite small. Females are less than 0.125 inch (3 mm) long. Males are even smaller—less than 0.04 inch (1 mm) long. If you see a flea at all, it just looks like a dark speck. But these tiny creatures can cause great suffering. Their bites are very itchy, and fleas can transmit diseases.

About 2,500 flea species exist around the world. These include the cat flea, dog flea, and human flea. Of these three species, the cat flea is the one found most often on dogs and people as well as cats.

12

THE BLACK DEATH

In 1348, a terrible disease arrived in Europe. Victims suffered fever, headache, weakness, fatigue, and painful swollen glands, and usually died within a week. People didn't know what caused it. They called it the plague or the Black Death. It's estimated that one-third to one-half of Europe's population died from it. Today, we know plague is caused by a **bacterium** carried by fleas found on certain rats. Plague is still around, but today it's easily treated with **antibiotics**.

A cat flea makes its way through the fur of an animal.

13

FABULOUS JUMPING FLEAS

Unlike most insects, fleas are wingless. They make up for this with amazing jumping skills. Their back legs are enlarged and have special stretchy pads to aid jumping. Their tiny size and remarkable jumping ability led to the creation of flea circuses, with fleas executing various tricks. Accounts of performing fleas go back to the late 1500s. So, how far can fleas jump? They can leap 13 inches (33 cm)—more than 100 times the length of their body!

A cat flea looks pretty scary under a microscope!

Fleas are extremely well adapted for their life of sucking blood. Their body is flat from side to side to make it easy to move through an animal's fur or feathers. Long claws on their legs also help them move around. Hairs and spines on their body and head help them stay in place even when an animal tries to groom them off.

The mouth is specially adapted for piercing skin and drinking blood. Mouthparts called laciniae (luh-SIH-nee-ee) cut through the skin. A needlelike epipharynx (eh-puh-FA-rinks) stabs the blood vessel. Saliva flows down the laciniae to keep the blood from clotting. Then, pumps in the mouth and gut go to work to suck in the blood. Each flea consumes 15 times its weight in blood each day!

DID YOU KNOW?

The tiny animals called water fleas aren't insects at all. They're crustaceans, like lobsters and crabs. Like insects, crustaceans have an exoskeleton, but most live in water and breathe through gills.

cat flea

NIBBLING
NO-SEE-UMS

Perhaps after spending time outside, you've discovered you have lots of extremely itchy, small red bites. You didn't see any bugs. What happened? Insects called no-see-ums may be responsible. They're called this because they're almost invisible. No-see-ums are also known as biting midges, gnats, and punkies. These tiny insects—less than 0.125 inch (3 mm) long—look and act like tiny mosquitoes. They have large compound eyes, a pair of antennae, and a proboscis. As with mosquitoes, females need blood for their eggs to develop. Inside the proboscis are long **mandibles** edged with teeth that are used to cut skin. The insect's saliva keeps the blood from clotting. Then the no-see-um sucks up the blood through her proboscis. She may feed for up to 5 minutes!

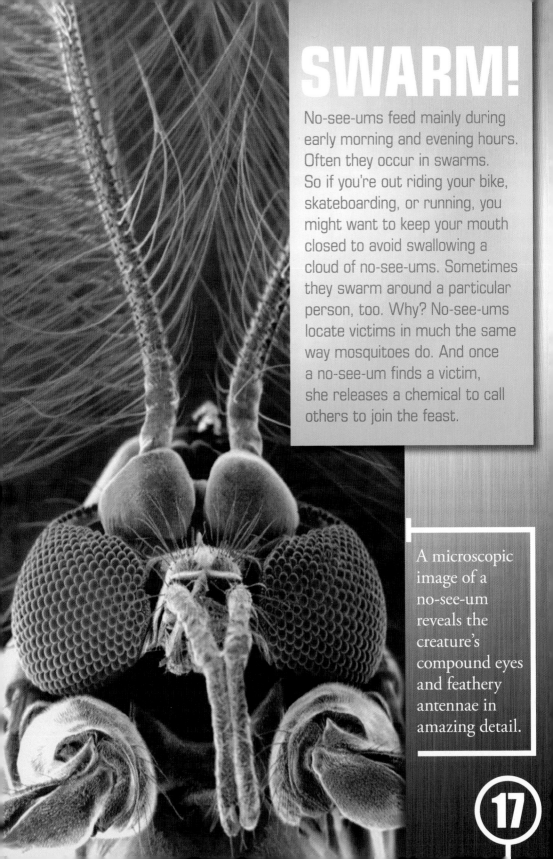

SWARM!

No-see-ums feed mainly during early morning and evening hours. Often they occur in swarms. So if you're out riding your bike, skateboarding, or running, you might want to keep your mouth closed to avoid swallowing a cloud of no-see-ums. Sometimes they swarm around a particular person, too. Why? No-see-ums locate victims in much the same way mosquitoes do. And once a no-see-um finds a victim, she releases a chemical to call others to join the feast.

A microscopic image of a no-see-um reveals the creature's compound eyes and feathery antennae in amazing detail.

MITE-Y CHIGGERS

DID YOU KNOW?

Your skin tries to protect itself from the chigger's saliva by forming a hard, tubelike structure around the liquid. But this just winds up acting like a straw for the chigger to use to suck up your dissolved cells.

If no-see-ums didn't cause the itchy bumps that appeared after you spent time outside, chiggers probably did. These invisible creatures are only about 0.007 inch (0.18 mm) long. If you viewed one through a microscope, you would think it was an insect since it has six legs. However, a chigger is really a mite in its larva stage. When it's grown, it will have eight legs like all arachnids. And it will feed mostly on plants.

Chiggers are red, but not because they suck blood. They use their short, delicate mouthparts to pierce areas of thin skin. A chemical in their saliva dissolves skin cells, and they drink the liquid. If a chigger doesn't get knocked off, it will continue to feed for 3 or 4 days!

18

ARACHNID
ASSASSINS

Another fascinating tiny arachnid is the **assassin** spider. These spiders are only about 0.08 inch (2 mm) long, but they can be deadly for other spiders. Assassin spiders stab their prey with **venom**-filled fangs located at the end of extremely long jaws. To support these long jaws, the spiders have developed a very long neck. These features make assassin spiders look pretty strange, but they allow the spiders to attack their prey without getting too close.

chigger

Some people believe that chiggers bury themselves in your skin. However, this isn't true.

19

LOUSY LICE

DID YOU KNOW?

Although it isn't common, lice and their eggs, called nits, are sometimes found on eyelashes and eyebrows.

Have you ever had the sensation that something is crawling around in your hair? Head lice can cause this feeling. These tiny parasites are about 0.125 inch (3 mm) long and live only on humans.

Like fleas, lice are wingless. But unlike fleas, lice can't jump. They can only crawl. Their legs have hook-like claws they use to grasp hair as they crawl.

Lice drink blood several times a day. Six pairs of hooks around their mouth are used to attach to skin. After piercing the skin with stylets, they pour saliva into the wound to keep the blood from clotting. Then they suck up blood using a pump in their throat. Although lice are born colorless, the blood quickly turns them reddish brown.

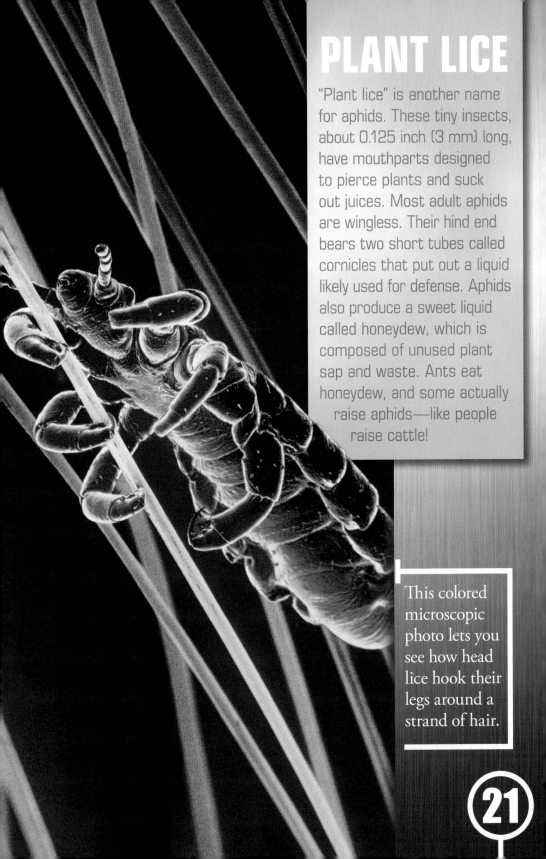

PLANT LICE

"Plant lice" is another name for aphids. These tiny insects, about 0.125 inch (3 mm) long, have mouthparts designed to pierce plants and suck out juices. Most adult aphids are wingless. Their hind end bears two short tubes called cornicles that put out a liquid likely used for defense. Aphids also produce a sweet liquid called honeydew, which is composed of unused plant sap and waste. Ants eat honeydew, and some actually raise aphids—like people raise cattle!

This colored microscopic photo lets you see how head lice hook their legs around a strand of hair.

SKIN EATERS

DID YOU KNOW?

One-tenth of the weight of a 2-year-old pillow may be composed of dead mites and their droppings.

You may not realize it, but your bed is a crowded place. It's home to tens of thousands—maybe millions—of dust mites. These little arachnids eat the skin flakes that people and their pets shed constantly. In fact, their scientific name is *Dermatophagoides*, which means "skin eater."

Dust mites are really tiny—just 0.01 inch (0.25 mm) long. They have long setae (SEE-tee), or hairs, along the edges of their body. Short setae cover the rest of the body and the legs. They have no eyes or antennae. They have no real head, either—just a group of mouthparts. They're among the creepiest-looking tiny bugs out there, but they're useful. Imagine the thick layer of skin flakes that would cover everything if it weren't for dust mites!

BEDTIME
BLOODSUCKERS

Dust mites may not be the only tiny creatures occupying your bed. There might also be bedbugs. These parasites are active at night and dine mainly on the blood of sleeping humans. They're flat, oval, wingless, reddish-brown insects about 0.2 inch (5 mm) long. Their piercing, sucking mouthparts fold to lie between their front legs. Adults feed for 10 to 15 minutes at a time. When they're full, they crawl away to a hiding place to **digest** their meal.

Dust mites, at left, also live in rugs, padded furniture, and pet beds. They don't transmit diseases, but they cause allergies in some people.

PANTRY PESTS

DID YOU KNOW?

Your cereal might also contain very tiny wingless insects called book lice or psocids (SOH-suhdz). Book lice eat only fungus or mold, so if they're in your cereal, it means mold is growing there!

Next time you have breakfast, you might discover you're not the only one who thought cereal sounded good. Numerous beetles and other insects feed on food products you might have at home.

Saw-toothed grain beetles, red flour beetles, and confused flour beetles are slender, flat, and dark red or brown. All feed on cereals, grains, and dried fruit. Saw-toothed grain beetles have a sweet tooth and will also snack on your candy.

Drugstore beetles are covered with small hairs. Their head is tucked down below the front of their body and can't be seen from above. In addition to grains and cereals, they eat spices, makeup, medicines, and even the poison strychnine! All these beetles are about 0.1 inch (2.5 mm) long.

FRUIT FLIES

Almost everyone has seen fruit flies in their kitchen. These tiny insects are about 0.125 inch (3 mm) long and usually have red eyes. They breed on ripe fruits and vegetables that aren't refrigerated, but they also breed in places you might not expect—drains, empty bottles and cans, trash containers, and even mops and cleaning rags! They're mostly just annoying, but they can spread bacteria.

Confused flour beetles like these are found in stored food all over the world.

EARTH ALERT!

DID YOU KNOW?

About one-third of our diet comes from plants pollinated by insects. And honeybees are responsible for 80 percent of all insect pollination!

Scientist first found *Varroa* mites in the United States in 1987. Adult female *Varroa* mites are shiny, reddish brown, shield shaped, and about 0.04 inch (1 mm) long and 0.06 inch (1.5 mm) wide. Males are about half that size.

Varroa mites feed on both adult honeybees and larvae. They pierce the insect's body, then suck out the juices. The mites have already killed almost all wild honeybees.

You may think fewer bees is a good thing. After all, their stings are painful and can even kill people who are allergic to them. But if all the honeybees die, our diet would change greatly. Honeybees give us more than honey. Many of the fruits and vegetables we eat wouldn't exist without the **pollination** carried out by honeybees.

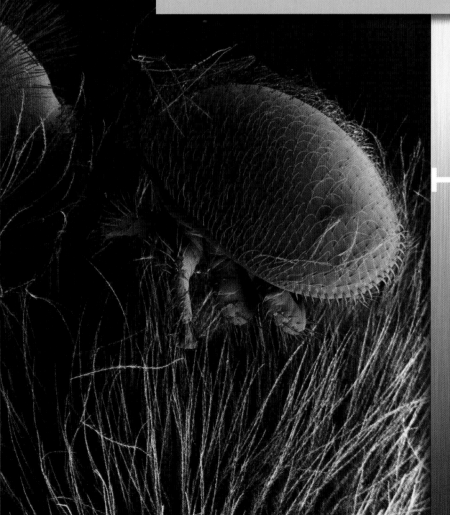

WILDFIRES AND TINY BEETLES

In 2012, wildfires raged across the western United States for months, burning tens of thousands of acres of forest. They destroyed homes and caused injuries and deaths. Extreme dryness after years of low rainfall made it easy for fire to spread. But another factor also contributed—mountain pine beetles. These tiny insects, about 0.125 inch (3 mm) long, feed on trees and spread deadly fungi to them. The dead, dry trees provided ready fuel for fires.

Because *Varroa* mites are flat, they can hide between the segments of a bee's body.

BENEFICIAL BUGS

DID YOU KNOW?

Whirligig beetles have two pairs of eyes. One pair is above the surface of the water, and one pair is below. This way, whirligigs can see what's happening above and below the water at the same time.

By now, you may think all tiny bugs are bad. But that's not true. Many are beneficial. Several kinds eat bugs that harm crops and other plants. Some return **nutrients** to the soil and help plants grow. Some even help keep water clean.

Ladybugs, or ladybird beetles, and minute pirate bugs are predators of plant-eating pests. Almost everyone is familiar with ladybugs. Minute pirate bugs eat both insect pests and their eggs.

Whirligig beetles swim in waterways and help keep them clean by eating dead or dying insects and debris.

These are just a few of the beneficial bugs in our world. Check out the chart on the next page to learn more about them and other tiny bug friends!

28

HELPFUL, ANNOYING MINUTE PIRATE BUGS

Farmers like minute pirate bugs because they eat insects that feed on corn, potatoes, and other crops. The bugs also dine on spider mites, which damage many garden vegetables, fruits, and flowers and harm some trees. Because minute pirate bugs are so good at getting rid of so many pests, people sometimes buy them to put among their crops or in their gardens. Unfortunately, in late summer, they can become minor pests themselves—they start biting people!

BENEFICIAL BUGS

name	size	appearance	benefits	fun fact
ladybugs, ladybird beetles, lady beetles	0.25 inch (6.4 mm)	round or oval; red or orange with black spots; short legs and antennae	eat aphids, mites, other plant-eating pests	can squeeze a bad-tasting liquid from leg joints
minute pirate bugs	0.125 inch (3 mm)	oval; black with white wing patches	eat aphids, spider mites, small caterpillars, insect eggs	can eat more than 30 spider mites in 1 day
parasitic Trichogramma wasps	0.01 inch (0.25 mm); some larger	black or brown with clear wings	lay their eggs in the eggs of more than 200 kinds of insect pests; wasp larvae eat host larvae	males are rare because the wasps carry a bacterium that kills males but not females
whirligig beetles	0.25 inch (6.4 mm); some larger	broad, flat black body with a fringe of hairs and orange legs	eat dead or dying insects and debris on the surface of waterways	carry an air bubble with them and use it to breathe underwater
springtails	0.04–0.08 inch (1–2 mm)	wingless; poor eyesight; special body part called furcula at rear end that's used for springing	return nutrients to soil by breaking down decaying plants, fungi, bacteria, and insect waste	1 cubic foot (0.03 cu m) of soil may be home to 50,000 springtails
predatory mites	0.02 inch (0.5 mm); some slightly larger	teardrop-shaped body; long legs; orange, red, tan, or brown	eat spider mites and eggs, and small insects and insect eggs	can recognize each other and tend to stick with mites they know

GLOSSARY

antibiotic: a drug that can kill germs, including harmful bacteria

assassin: a creature that kills others of its kind

bacterium: a tiny creature that can only be seen with a microscope. More than one bacterium are called bacteria.

carbon dioxide: a gas breathed out by animals

digest: to break down food inside the body so that the body can use it

environment: the conditions that surround a living thing and affect the way it lives

exoskeleton: the hard outer covering of an animal's body

lactic acid: a substance produced by the body as a result of the breakdown of sugars during exercise

mandible: a mouthpart of insects or arachnids used to bite or hold food

nutrient: something a living thing needs to grow and stay alive

parasitic: living in or on another organism, usually causing it harm

pollination: the transfer of plant pollen that results in fruits and vegetables

quadrillion: 1,000,000,000,000,000, or 1 million billions

venom: poisonous matter created by an animal and passed on by a bite or sting

FOR MORE INFORMATION

BOOKS

Mound, Laurence. *Insect*. New York, NY: DK Publishing, 2007.

PlayBac Publishing. *Incredible Insects! Eye-Opening Photos of Amazing Bugs*. New York, NY: PlayBac Publishing, 2009.

Schlitt, Christine. *Journey into the Invisible: The World from Under the Microscope*. New York, NY: Sky Pony Press, 2013.

Townsend, John. *Incredible Arachnids*. Chicago, IL: Raintree, 2006.

WEBSITES

BioKids: Arachnids
www.biokids.umich.edu/critters/Arachnida/
Read about arachnids and see some awesome pictures.

BrainPop: Arachnids
www.brainpop.com/science/diversityoflife/arachnids/preview.weml
Watch a movie to find out about arachnids.

Insects
kids.sandiegozoo.org/animals/insects
Learn what features make a creature an insect, then click on pictures to learn more about specific insects.

INDEX

antennae 7, 10, 11, 16, 17, 22, 29

aphids 21, 29

arachnids 7, 18, 19, 22

assassin spider 19

bedbugs 23

beneficial bugs 28, 29

blood 8, 9, 10, 11, 15, 16, 18, 20, 23

book lice 24

chiggers 18, 19

compound eyes 10, 11, 16, 17

confused flour beetles 24, 25

diseases 8, 12, 13, 23

drugstore beetles 24

dust mites 22, 23

epipharynx 15

fairy flies 6

flea circuses 14

fleas 12, 13, 14, 15, 20

fruit flies 25

head lice 20, 21

insects 4, 5, 6, 7, 8, 9, 11, 14, 15, 16, 18, 21, 23, 24, 25, 26, 27, 28, 29

laciniae 15

ladybugs 28, 29

mandibles 16

minute pirate bugs 28, 29

mites 7, 18, 29

mosquitoes 8, 9, 10, 11, 16, 17

mountain pine beetles 27

nits 20

no-see-ums 16, 17, 18

parasite 6, 12, 20, 23

plague 13

plant lice 21

proboscis 10, 11, 16

psocids 24

red flour beetles 24

saliva 11, 15, 16, 18, 20

saw-toothed grain beetles 24

skin flakes 22

stylets 11, 20

Varroa mites 26, 27

whirligig beetles 28, 29

wings 6, 7, 8, 9, 29